To our kids, Miles, Hayden, and Dorothy, and our favorite
meatball-loving dog, Jake Bacon Florence —tf

To Daniele and Drew —cf

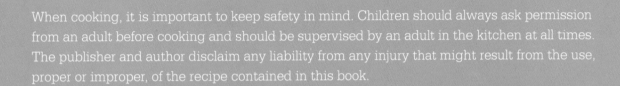

When cooking, it is important to keep safety in mind. Children should always ask permission
from an adult before cooking and should be supervised by an adult in the kitchen at all times.
The publisher and author disclaim any liability from any injury that might result from the use,
proper or improper, of the recipe contained in this book.

Tyler Makes Spaghetti!
Text copyright © 2013 by Tyler Florence
Illustrations copyright © 2013 by Craig Frazier
All rights reserved. Manufactured in China.
No part of this book may be used or reproduced in any manner whatsoever without
written permission except in the case of brief quotations embodied in critical articles
and reviews. For information address HarperCollins Children's Books, a division of
HarperCollins Publishers, 10 East 53rd Street, New York, NY 10022.
www.harpercollinschildrens.com

———

Library of Congress Cataloging-in-Publication Data is available.
ISBN 978-0-06-204756-4

———

The artist created the illustrations with pen and ink and colored them digitally.
Typography by Craig Frazier
13 14 15 16 17   SCP   10 9 8 7 6 5 4 3 2 1

❖
First Edition

Tyler

MAKES SPAGHETTI!

WRITTEN BY
Tyler Florence

ILLUSTRATED BY
Craig Frazier

HARPER
An Imprint of HarperCollinsPublishers

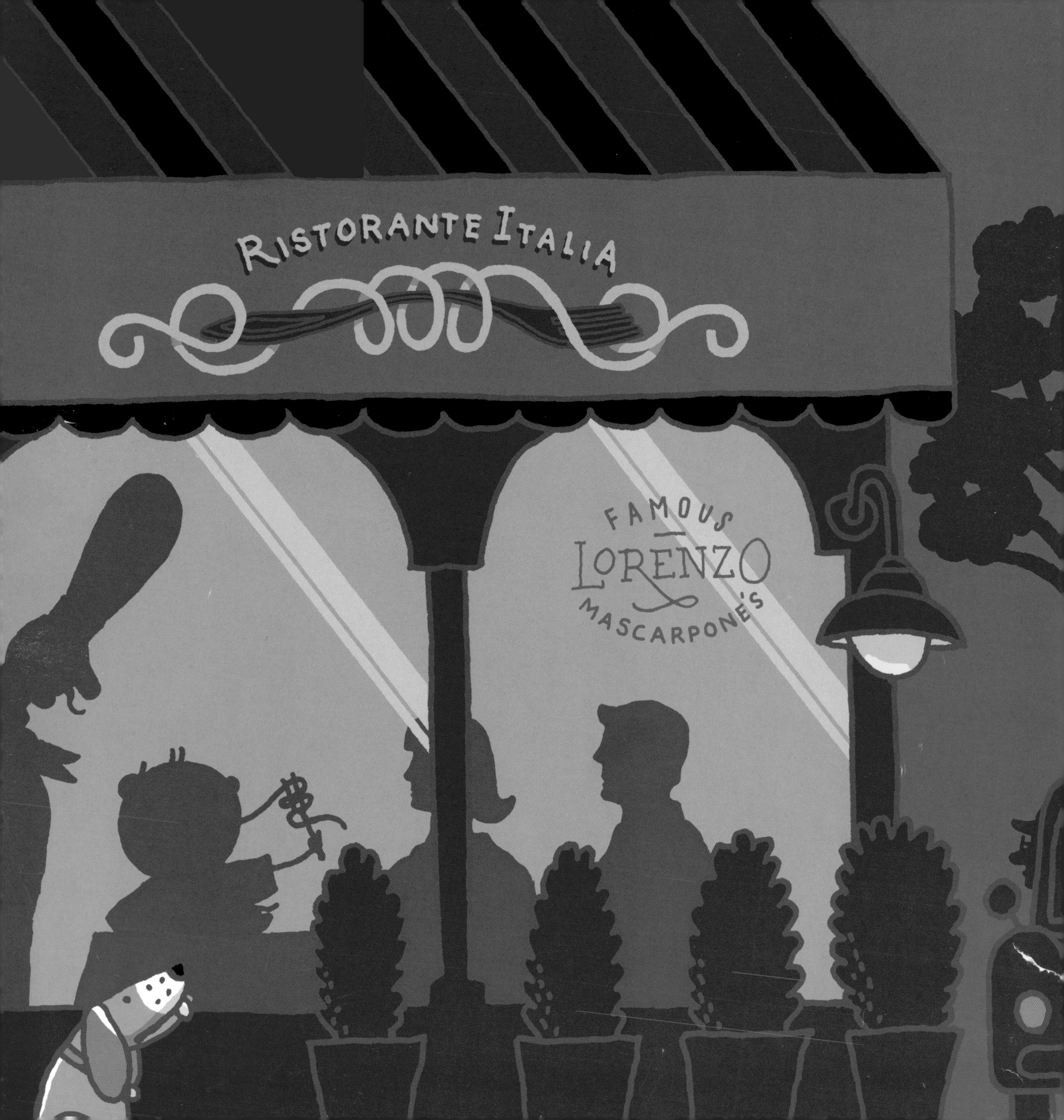
RISTORANTE ITALIA
FAMOUS
LORENZO
MASCARPONE'S

Tyler and his family were at their favorite restaurant. The chef came by to say hello.

"*Buon giorno*. Welcome back!" he said. "Tyler, I see you've ordered your usual."

"Spaghetti and meatballs is my favorite, Chef!" said Tyler. "I could eat it every day!"

"Well, that's good," said Chef, "because I'm making more tomorrow—and I could use your help."

"Really?" said Tyler. "I'll be here!"

The next morning, Tyler zoomed over to the restaurant.

"I can't believe Chef Lorenzo is going to show me how to make my favorite recipe. I'm going to make spaghetti and meatballs for dinner tonight!"

"It will smell even better when we make our spaghetti and meatballs," said Chef. "We'll need pasta, tomatoes, olive oil, onions, garlic, meatballs, parmesan cheese, and basil. Let's start!"

"It smells delicious in here," said Tyler when he walked into Chef Lorenzo's kitchen.

"First we make the pasta dough. We use a special flour called semolina from Italy. It makes pasta nice and chewy. Then we add a few eggs, a little olive oil, and salt," said Chef.

"I know how to crack an egg, Chef," Tyler said.

"*Perfetto*," said Chef.

"Next we roll the dough out into paper-thin sheets."

"It looks like a pasta cape," said Tyler.

"Being a good cook is sort of like being a superhero," said Chef Lorenzo. "Good food can save the day!"

"The next thing we do is cut the sheets into noodles. There are lots of different shapes of pasta—like macaroni, fettuccine, and linguine. But right now we're making your favorite."

"Spaghetti!" yelled Tyler.

"It looks like Tofu is getting his pasta to go!" said Chef. "Let's go on an adventure for the rest of the ingredients. Just imagine…"

"Wow! What are we here for?" asked Tyler.

"Your favorite spaghetti has tomato sauce, so we need big, juicy tomatoes!"

"Chef?" Tyler asked. "Are the tomatoes in your sauce the same kind that I put on my sandwich?"

"Yes, Tyler, they are," answered Chef. "Great tomatoes come from all over the world—Italy, California, and even New Jersey.

"The longer they are left on the vine, the better they taste for my sauce and your sandwich, too," said Chef.

"What else do we need?" asked Tyler.

"Have you ever tasted fresh basil?" asked Chef. "It has a very sweet flavor and makes the sauce super yummy. I grow it in my own garden."

"Hey, Chef, look! I can make a
mustache out of it—just like yours!"
said Tyler.

"What's next?"

"Oooh, what's so stinky here?" asked Tyler.

"Onions and garlic!" said Chef. "They can be a little stinky when they're raw, but chopped up and cooked in olive oil, they taste sweet and delicious."

"What else?" asked Tyler.

"Olive oil," said Chef. "It's one of the oldest ingredients in the world. It comes from smashing lots and lots of ripe olives."

"How does oil come out of this tiny olive?" asked Tyler.

"Some places use special machines, but in some towns they still do it the old-fashioned way, with a giant stone wheel," said Chef Lorenzo.

"Cool! What's next?" asked Tyler.

"That's it for the ingredients that go *into* the sauce, but now we need the cheese that goes on top," said Chef.

"Cheese comes from milk, right?" asked Tyler.

"Yes, but this is not just any cheese: this is Parmigiano-Reggiano. We call it Parmesan for short. Now, that's *amore*," said Chef. "I think we have everything we need."

"Now it's time to cook!" said Chef.

"Okay, but just don't say that word," said Tyler.

"What word?" asked Chef Lorenzo.

"M-e-a-t-b-a-l-l-s," Tyler whispered. "Tofu goes crazy for them!"

But it was too late. Tofu jumped up and knocked the bowl of meatballs out of Chef's hands.

"Wow! Tofu could win first place in a meatball-eating contest," said Chef.

"Let's get out of here, Tofu," said Tyler. "We've worn out our welcome, and you've eaten way too many meatballs."

"You have everything you need, Tyler…tomatoes, pasta, meatballs, basil, and cheese," said Chef.

"Ciao, and have fun cooking dinner tonight. Don't let that dog eat it all—he's a sneaky one."

"Thank you, Chef, for teaching me how to make my favorite dish in the world," said Tyler.

At home, Tyler and his dad start making the tomato sauce. They sauté finely chopped onions and garlic in olive oil until soft. Next they add the tomatoes and simmer until thick and delicious. When Tofu isn't looking, they add the meatballs.

Then they boil up the spaghetti that Tyler and Chef Lorenzo made. Tofu does a taste test to make sure it's done.

With pasta, meatballs, and tomato sauce
piled high, Tyler walks his masterpiece to
the table. *Bellissimo*!

"Chef Lorenzo! I didn't know you were coming over for dinner," Tyler exclaimed.

"I hear there is a new chef in town making spaghetti and meatballs, Tyler. I had to come and try them. Let's eat!" said Chef.

Tyler passed around the Parmesan, and everyone sprinkled some on top of their pasta.

"What do you think?" asked Tyler after taking a bite.

"Magnifico," said Chef. "I think you've earned your own chef's coat!"

"Bravo!" said Tyler. "Now I look like a real chef."

"What's next, Tyler?" Chef asked.

"Tofu's birthday." said Tyler. "I think I'll make him a super-duper birthday cake!"

TYLER'S SPAGHETTI
AND MEATBALLS
RECIPE

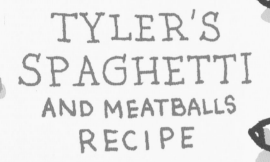

Meatballs:

Extra virgin olive oil

1 onion, chopped

2 garlic cloves, smashed

2 tablespoons roughly chopped fresh parsley leaves

1 cup milk

4 thick slices firm white bread, crust removed

1½ pounds ground beef

1 large egg

½ cup freshly grated Parmigiano-Reggiano, also known
   as Parmesan, plus more for serving

Kosher salt and freshly ground black pepper

4 cups heated tomato sauce (recipe follows) or good-
   quality jarred tomato sauce

Fresh basil leaves for garnish

Spaghetti:

1 pound uncooked spaghetti

Tomato Sauce:

½ cup extra virgin olive oil

1 medium onion, chopped

3 garlic cloves, chopped

2 (28-ounce) cans whole peeled San Marzano tomatoes,
   drained and crushed by hand, liquid reserved

Kosher salt and freshly ground black pepper

¼ cup fresh basil leaves, torn into pieces

Heat the olive oil in a large saucepan over medium-low
   heat. Add the onion and garlic and cook until the
   vegetables are soft, 4 to 5 minutes. Carefully add the
   tomatoes (nothing splashes like tomatoes) and about
   ½ cup of the reserved liquid, and season with salt and
   pepper. Cook until the sauce is thick, about 15 minutes.
   Taste and adjust seasoning with salt and pepper. Bring
   to a boil, stirring for a few minutes with a wooden
   spoon to further break up the tomatoes. Reduce the
   heat and let simmer for 20 to 25 minutes. Stir in the
   fresh basil and season again.

Yield: 4 cups

Directions:

Bring a big pot of salted water to a boil for the spaghetti.
Heat 3 tablespoons oil in a skillet over medium heat.
Add the onion, garlic, and parsley and cook until the
vegetables are soft but still translucent, about 10 minutes.
Take the pan off the heat and let cool.

Pour enough milk over the bread in a bowl to moisten
and let it soak while the onions are cooling. In a separate
bowl, combine the meat, egg, and Parmesan, and season
generously with salt and pepper. Use your hands to
squeeze the excess milk out of the bread and add that to
the bowl along with the cooled onion mixture. (Hang on
to the pan—you'll need it to cook the meatballs.) Gently
combine all the ingredients with your hands or with a
spoon until just mixed together. Don't overwork or the
meatballs will be tough. Divide into 10 equal pieces and
shape them into 10 nice-looking meatballs.

Preheat the oven to 350 degrees F.

Heat a quarter cup of olive oil in the frying pan over
medium heat and brown the meatballs on all sides, about
10 minutes. Put them into a baking dish and spoon about
half of the tomato sauce over. Put the meatballs in the
oven and bake until the meatballs are cooked through,
about 15 minutes.

Meanwhile, cook the spaghetti in the boiling water until
al dente, about 8 minutes. Drain and put it onto a large
serving platter. Pour on the rest of the sauce and mix
well. Spoon the meatballs on top of the spaghetti and
garnish with basil leaves. Serve immediately
along with extra cheese.

Parmesan cheese is an Italian cheese made from cow's milk. Real Parmigiano-Reggiano comes from only one place in Italy called Emilia-Romagna. It takes about two years to age and is made in really big "wheels" that weigh up to one hundred pounds! They are cut into smaller "wedges" so they will fit in your refrigerator!

Basil is an herb that belongs to the mint family and has a fragrant and sweet taste. The leaf is the part of the plant that is harvested and used as a flavoring herb to many meals. It is best friends with garlic and onions in lots of Italian recipes.

Did You Know?

Onions and garlic are from the lilac family of plants and grow under the ground. They both have very strong smells. Garlic is even called "the stinking rose." Onions smell so strong that they can make you cry when you cut them. But both onions and garlic are known for the yummy flavors they bring to foods.

Pasta is made from eggs and flour and comes in many shapes—like elbows, wagon wheels, shells, spirals, and spaghetti. Fresh pasta is soft, but if you dry it, it becomes very hard and brittle until it is boiled. Dry pasta takes about 12 minutes of boiling to become all soft and "noodley."

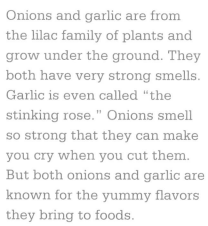

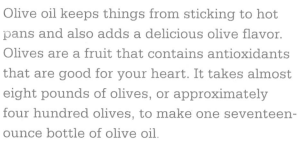

Olive oil keeps things from sticking to hot pans and also adds a delicious olive flavor. Olives are a fruit that contains antioxidants that are good for your heart. It takes almost eight pounds of olives, or approximately four hundred olives, to make one seventeen-ounce bottle of olive oil.

Most people think tomatoes are vegetables, but they are actually fruit! They are a great source of vitamins A and C. They are sweet in taste and can be eaten raw in salads or cooked to make soup or deep-red sauces like on spaghetti. Ketchup is made from tomatoes.